The Christian and Prayer

Unlocking the Secrets of a Successful Prayer Life

STEP 4

Bill Bright

NewLife
PUBLICATIONS
A MINISTRY OF CAMPUS CRUSADE FOR CHRIST

Ten Basic Steps Toward Christian Maturity
Step 4: The Christian and Prayer

Published by
New*Life* Publications
100 Sunport Lane
Orlando, FL 32809

Printed in the United States of America.

ISBN: 1-56399-033-4

Thomas Nelson Inc., Nashville, Tennessee, is the exclusive distributor of this book to the trade markets in the United States and the District of Columbia.

Distributed in Canada by Campus Crusade for Christ of Canada, Surrey, B.C.

Unless otherwise indicated, all Scripture references are from the *New International Version*, © 1973, 1978, 1984 by the International Bible Society. Published by Zondervan Bible Publishers, Grand Rapids, Michigan.

Scripture quotations designated TLB are from *The Living Bible*, © 1971 by Tyndale House Publishers, Wheaton, Illinois.

Scripture quotations designated NASB are from the *New American Standard Bible*, © 1960, 1962, 1963, 1968, 1971, 1972, 1973, 1975, 1977 by the Lockman Foundation, La Habra, California.

Scripture quotations designated NKJ are from the *New King James* version, © 1979, 1980, 1982 by Thomas Nelson Inc., Publishers, Nashville, Tennessee.

NewLife2000 is a registered service mark of Campus Crusade for Christ, Inc.

Any royalties from this book or the many other books by Bill Bright are dedicated to the glory of God and designated to the various ministries of Campus Crusade for Christ/*NewLife2000*.

For more information, write:

L.I.F.E.—P. O. Box 40, Flemmington Markets, 2129, Australia
Campus Crusade for Christ of Canada—Box 300, Vancouver, B.C., V6C 2X3, Canada
Campus Crusade for Christ—Fairgate House, King's Road, Tyseley, Birmingham, B11 2AA, England
Lay Institute for Evangelism—P. O. Box 8786, Auckland 3, New Zealand
Campus Crusade for Christ—Alexandra, P. O. Box 0205, Singapore 9115, Singapore
Great Commission Movement of Nigeria—P. O. Box 500, Jos, Plateau State Nigeria, West Africa
Campus Crusade for Christ International—100 Sunport Lane, Orlando, FL 32809, USA

Contents

Acknowledgments

The *Ten Basic Steps Toward Christian Maturity* series was a product of necessity. As the ministry of Campus Crusade for Christ expanded rapidly to scores of campuses across America, thousands of students committed their lives to Christ—several hundred on a single campus. Individual follow-up of all new converts soon became impossible. Who was to help them grow in their new-found faith?

A Bible study series designed for new Christians was desperately needed—a study that would stimulate individuals and groups to explore the depths and the riches of God's Word. Although several excellent studies were available, we felt the particular need of new material for these college students.

In 1955, I asked several of my fellow staff associates to assist me in the preparation of Bible studies that would stimulate both evangelism and Christian growth in a new believer. The contribution by campus staff members was especially significant because of their constant contact with students in introducing them to Christ and meeting regularly with them to disciple them. Thus, the *Ten Basic Steps Toward Christian Maturity* was the fruit of our combined labor.

Since that modest beginning, many other members of the staff have contributed generously. On occasion, for example, I found myself involved in research and writing sessions with several of our staff, all seminary graduates, some with advanced degrees and one with his doctorate in theology. More important, all were actively engaged in "winning, building, and sending men" for Christ.

For this latest edition, I want to thank Don Tanner for his professional assistance in revising, expanding, and editing the contents. I also want to thank Joette Whims and Jean Bryant for their extensive help and for joining Don and me in the editorial process.

A Personal Word

As Founder and President of Campus Crusade for Christ, I have the privilege of working with nearly 50,000 full-time dedicated staff, associate staff, and trained volunteers in all the major countries representing 98 percent of the world's population. We work with millions of Christians around the world and are seeing tens of millions receive Christ as their Savior and Lord.

As of this printing, we have helped to train millions of Christians of all denominations. Together we have helped to present the gospel to an estimated one-and-a-half billion people (864 million of whom have been documented). The film "JESUS," which we sponsored and financed, has been viewed by almost 550 million people in 255 languages.

Our goal is to help reach more than six billion people with the gospel of our Lord Jesus Christ and help fulfill the Great Commission by the year 2000. Millions of Christians in thousands of churches of all major denominations are involved in this worldwide master strategy called *NewLife2000®*.

The strategy calls for presenting the gospel through 10,000 "JESUS" Film teams and other effective evangelistic tools, helping participating denominations plant one million new churches, launching ministries on thousands of campuses in strategic metropolitan areas worldwide, and establishing five to twenty million *New Life Groups* (more than 200,000 have already been started throughout the world).

But one day I fully expect God will promote me to a far more important responsibility, and that is to a ministry of full-time prayer.

There is absolutely nothing more important in the believer's life than prayer. Has it ever occurred to you that you can be used of God to literally help change the lives of men and nations? God has made available to us in prayer a vast reservoir of power, wisdom, and grace—if only we are willing to claim His promises by faith.

The New Testament records many passages that suggest prayer played a major role in evangelism and discipleship in the early church. The same is true for today. On one occasion, for example, five high school students began to sense their responsibility to God in helping to fulfill the Great Commission on their campus. Each was impressed to name three friends he wanted to claim for Christ.

The first week they met daily to pray that these friends would sense their need of the Savior. The second week they prayed to be instruments of God. And the third week they prayed for opportunities to speak to their friends about Christ. That week all fifteen students for whom they had prayed received the Savior.

Prayer is the primary means of becoming a fruitful witness for Christ. The divine order is: first talk to God about men and then talk to men about God. Witnessing is harvesting the results of prayer.

It is very important that early in your Christian life you understand the value and blessings of sincere prayer. Not only does it produce fruitfulness, it is the major path to fellowship with our Father. The amazing fact, revealed through God's holy Word, is that He desires our fellowship. It gives Him great pleasure when we choose to spend time with Him in fellowship and prayer.

Would you like to experience a vibrant and effective prayer life? I have prepared this study to help you develop and maintain a fruitful life of prayer. I urge you to study each lesson carefully and prayerfully. God bless you as you learn how to be a powerful prayer warrior for the Lord Jesus.

What This Study Will Do for You

Ihave observed through the years that the average Christian does not know how to pray.

A friend of mine who has been a Christian for more than fifty years told me, "I never pray in public, and I know very little about prayer or how to pray." Because so many Christians—new and old alike—know so little about prayer, I want to share with you some simple, basic truths and answer some vital questions about prayer.

You will benefit from this study in four ways:

First, *by learning the true purpose of prayer.* God waits anxiously for you to come to Him in prayer. Proverbs 15:8 says, "The prayer of the upright is His delight" (NKJ). In this study, you will learn why prayer is God's appointed way of doing His work.

Second, *by understanding the roles of the Father, Son, and Holy Spirit in your prayer.* It is meaningful and encouraging to know that when we pray to our heavenly Father, our prayers are accepted by Jesus Christ and interpreted to God the Father by the Holy Spirit. In this study, you will learn how each person in the Godhead works together to bring about the answers to your prayers.

Third, *by learning how to pray effectively.* God is more interested in our hearts than in

Studying the lessons will help you develop a consistent and effective daily prayer life.

our words when we pray. But the Bible gives us clear guidelines on how to approach God. Studying the lessons will help you apply these principles and develop a consistent and effective daily prayer life.

Fourth, *by discovering how to use the great power available through prayer.* Prayer is not only the greatest privilege of the Christian life, but the most revolutionary source of power known to man. This study will show you how to claim God's promises concerning prayer and tap into this power.

Foundation for Faith

Step 4: The Christian and Prayer is part of the *Ten Basic Steps Toward Christian Maturity,* a time-tested study series designed to provide you with a sure foundation for your faith. Hundreds of thousands have benefited from this Bible study series during the almost forty years since it was first published in its original form.

When you complete Step 4, I encourage you to continue your study with the rest of the Steps.

If you are a new Christian, the *Ten Basic Steps* will acquaint you with the major doctrines of the Christian faith. By applying the principles you will learn, you will grow spiritually and find solutions to problems you are likely to face as a new believer.

If you are a mature Christian, you will discover the tools you need to help others receive Christ and grow in their faith. Your own commitment to our Lord will be affirmed, and you will discover how to develop an effective devotional and study plan.

The series includes an individual booklet for the introductory study and one for each of the ten Steps. These study guides correlate with the expanded and updated *Handbook for Christian Maturity* and *Ten Basic Steps Leader's Guide.*

Each Step reveals a different facet of the Christian life and truth, and each contains lessons for study that can be used during your personal quiet time or in a group setting.

I encourage you to pursue the study of Step 4 with an open, eager mind. As you read, continually pray that God will show you how to relate the principles you learn to your own situation. Begin to apply them on a daily basis, and you will make the wonderful discovery of a Spirit-empowered prayer life.

How to Use This Study

On page 12 of this Step, you will find the preparatory article, "Discovering the Secret of Successful Prayer." The article will give you a clear perspective on how you can release the power of prayer in your life and ministry. Read it carefully before you begin Lesson 1. Review it prayerfully during your study.

This Step contains six lessons plus a "Recap" or review. Each lesson is divided into two sections: the Bible Study and the Life Application. Begin by noting the Objective for the lesson you are studying. The Objective states the main goal for your study. Keep it in mind as you continue through the lesson.

Take time to memorize the referenced Scripture verses. Learn each verse by writing it on a small card to carry with you. You can buy cards for these verses at any bookstore or print shop, or you can make your own by using filing cards. Review daily the verses you have memorized.

Our Lord has commanded that we learn His Word. Proverbs 7:1–3 reminds us:

> My son, keep my words and store up my commands within you. Keep my commands and you will live; guard my teachings as the apple of your eye. Bind them on your fingers; write them on the tablet of your heart.

Your most important objective is not to accumulate knowledge, but to meet with God in a loving, personal way.

As you meditate on the verses you have memorized and claim God's promises, you will experience the joy, victory, and power that God's Word gives to your Christian walk. When you have finished all the studies in the entire series, you will be able to develop your own Bible study, continuing to use a systematic method for memorizing God's Word.

How to Study the Lessons

Casual Bible reading uncovers valuable spiritual facts that lie near the surface. But understanding the deeper truths requires study. Often the difference between reading and studying is a pen and notepad.

Every lesson in this study covers an important topic and gives you an opportunity to record your answers to the questions. Plan to spend a minimum of thirty minutes each day—preferably in the morning—in Bible study, meditation, and prayer.

Remember, the most important objective and benefit of a quiet time or Bible study is not to acquire knowledge or accumulate biblical information but to meet with God in a loving, personal way.

Here are some suggestions to help you in your study time:

◆ Plan a specific time and place to work on these studies. Make an appointment with God; then keep it.

◆ Have a pen or pencil, your Bible, and this booklet.

◆ Begin with prayer for God's presence, blessing, and wisdom.

◆ Meditate on the Objective to determine how it fits into your circumstances.

◆ Memorize the suggested verses.

◆ Proceed to the Bible study, trusting God to use it to teach you. Prayerfully anticipate His presence with you. Work carefully, reading the Scripture passages and thinking through the questions. Answer each as completely as possible.

◆ When you come to the Life Application, answer the questions honestly and begin to apply them to your own life.

◆ Prayerfully read through the lesson again and reevaluate your Life Application answers. Do they need changing? Or adjusting?

◆ Review the memory verses.

◆ Consider the Objective again and determine if it has been accomplished. If not, what do you need to do?

◆ Close with a prayer of thanksgiving and ask God to help you grow spiritually in the areas He has specifically revealed to you.

◆ When you complete the first six lessons of this Step, spend some extra time on the Recap to make sure you understand every lesson thoroughly.

◆ If you need more study of this Step, ask God for wisdom again and go through whatever lesson(s) you need to review, repeating the process until you do understand and are able to apply the truths to your own life.

These studies are not intended as a complete development of Christian beliefs. However, a careful study of the material will give you, with God's help, a sufficient understanding of how you can know and apply God's plan for your life.

By applying the spiritual truths contained here, you will gain greater confidence in the power of prayer, for God's holy Word promises, "This is the assurance we have in approaching God: that if we ask anything according to his will, he hears us. And if we know that he hears us—whatever we ask—we know that we have what we asked of him" (1 John 5:14,15).

Do not rush through the lessons. Take plenty of time to think through the questions. Meditate on them. Absorb the truths presented and make the application a part of your life. Give God a chance to speak to you, and let the Holy Spirit teach you. As you spend time with our Lord in prayer and study, you will experience the amazing joy of His presence (John 14:21).

Discovering the Secret of Successful Prayer

The story is told of a man who traveled to a certain city one cold morning. As he arrived at his hotel, he noticed that the clerks, the guests—everyone—was barefooted. In the coffee shop, he noticed an attractive fellow at a nearby table and asked, "Why aren't you wearing shoes? Don't you know about shoes?"

"Of course I know about shoes," the patron replied.

"Then why don't you wear them?" the visitor asked.

"Ah, that is the question," the patron returned. "Why don't I wear shoes?"

After breakfast, the visitor walked out of the hotel and into the snow. Again, every person he saw was barefooted. Curious, he asked a passerby, "Why doesn't anyone here wear shoes? Don't you know that they protect the feet from the cold?"

The passerby said, "We know about shoes. See that building? It's a shoe factory. We are so proud of the plant that we gather there every week to hear the man in charge tell us how wonderful shoes are."

"Then why don't you wear shoes?" the visitor persisted.

"Ah, that is the question," the passerby replied. "Why don't we wear shoes?"

God invites us to come before Him boldly in prayer with a reverent, joyful heart.

When it comes to prayer, many Christians are like the people in that city. They know about prayer, they believe in its power, they frequently hear sermons on the subject, but it is not a vital part of their lives.

In my study of God's Word and in my travels throughout the world, I have become absolutely convinced that wherever people really pray according to biblical principles, God works in their lives and through them in the lives of others in a special way. Show me a church or a Christian organization that emphasizes prayer, and I'll show you a ministry where people are excited about Jesus Christ and are witnessing for Him. On the other hand, show me a church or Christian cause where there is little emphasis on prayer, and I will show you worldly Christians who have little interest in the souls of men and women. Their lives can best be described by the experience of the Church of Ephesus (Revelation 2) and the Church of Laodicea (Revelation 3).

As we consider the secret of successful prayer, let me answer six vital questions.

What Is Prayer?

Simply put, prayer is communicating with God. As a child of God you are invited to come boldly before His throne. "Since we have a great high priest who has gone through the heavens, Jesus the Son of God," the apostle Paul writes, ". . . let us then approach the throne of grace with confidence, so that we may receive mercy and find grace to help us in our time of need" (Hebrews 4:14–16).

Because of who God is—the King of kings and the Lord of lords, the Creator of heaven and earth—we must come into His presence with reverence. But He is also our loving heavenly Father who cares for us and delights in having fellowship with us. Therefore, we can come to Him with a reverent, joyful heart, knowing He loves us more than anyone else has ever loved us or will ever love us.

Someone has said, "Prayer is the creator as well as the channel of devotion. The spirit of devotion is the spirit of prayer. Prayer and devotion are united as soul and body are united, as life and heart are united. There is no real prayer without devotion, no devotion without prayer." Real prayer is expressing our devotion to our heavenly Father, inviting Him to talk to us as we talk to Him.

Who Can Pray?

Anyone can pray, but only those who walk in faith and obedience to Christ can expect to receive answers to their prayers. Jesus says, "I am the way and the truth and the life. No one comes to the Father except through me" (John 14:6). Contact with God begins when we receive Jesus into our lives as Savior and Lord.

Praying with a clean heart also is vital to successful prayer. The psalmist says, "If I had cherished sin in my heart, the Lord would not have listened" (Psalm 66:18). We cannot expect God to answer our prayers if there is any unconfessed sin in our life.

One of the most frequent hindrances to prayer is an unforgiving spirit. Jesus says, "When you stand praying, if you hold anything against anyone, forgive him, so that your Father in heaven may forgive you your sins" (Mark 11:25). No prayer except the prayer of confession can be answered by God unless it comes from a heart that is free of unforgiveness and bitterness. You and I must come to God with a forgiving heart if we are to receive the Christian's legacy of power in prayer.

In addition, we must have a believing heart if we expect God to answer our prayers. Jesus says, "If you believe, you will receive whatever you ask for in prayer" (Matthew 21:22), and "According to your faith will it be done to you" (Matthew 9:29). Yet few of us take these words seriously, and few dare to claim what God has so generously promised us.

Why Are We to Pray?

God commands us to pray. The New Testament commands to pray are many. Here are a few: Watch and pray (Luke 21:36; Mark 14:38). Pray with thanksgiving (Philippians 4:6; Colossians 4:2). Pray in the Spirit (1 Corinthians 14:15). Always pray and not give up (Luke 18:1).

We also pray to have fellowship with God. Prayer is not just an "escape hatch" for us to get out of trouble, please ourselves, or gain our selfish ends. It is our "hotline" of communication and fellowship with God. In the process, we receive spiritual nurture and strength to live a victorious life, and we maintain the boldness necessary for a vital witness for Christ.

Genuine, biblically-based prayer does change things. It so transforms those who pray that God is free to reveal His will to them. Prayer also releases God's great power to change the course of nature, people, and nations. The faithful prayers of Spirit-filled believers have proven this throughout the Bible and history.

To Whom Do We Pray?

We pray to the Father in the name of the Lord Jesus Christ through the ministry of the Holy Spirit. When we pray to the Father, our prayers are accepted by Jesus Christ and interpreted to God the Father by the Holy Spirit.

But because God is one God, manifested in three persons, and since there is no jealously between the three persons of the Trinity, it is perfectly acceptable to pray to Jesus or to the Holy Spirit.

As we pray, both Jesus and the Holy Spirit are interceding on our behalf. Paul records in Romans 8:34, "Christ Jesus, who died—more than that, who was raised to life—is at the right hand of God and is also interceding for us." Earlier in that chapter, Paul wrote, "The Spirit helps us in our weakness... And he who searches our hearts knows the mind of the Spirit, because the Spirit intercedes for the saints in accordance with God's will" (verse 26,27).

When Should We Pray?

God's Word commands us to "Pray continually" (1 Thessalonians 5:17).

Charles Spurgeon said, "Prayer pulls the rope down below, and the great bell rings above in the ears of God. Some scarcely stir the bell, for they pray so languidly; others give only an occasional jerk at the rope. But he who communicates with heaven is the man who grasps the rope boldly and pulls continuously with all his might."

We can be in prayer frequently throughout the day, demonstrating our devotion to God as we go about our daily tasks.

I have found it meaningful to begin every morning in prayer. As I get out of bed, I fall on my knees to worship Him as a way of saying, "Lord, I bow before You and acknowledge You as my Master."

Throughout the day, I focus my thoughts on the Lord, often talking to Him, praising Him, and thanking Him for His goodness, love, and grace in my behalf. I pray for wisdom about the numerous decisions I must make each day. I pray for the salvation of friends and strangers, the healing of the sick, and the spiritual and material needs of Campus Crusade for Christ and other ministries. I even pray that the way I dress, as well as my words and actions, will bring glory to God. I ask Him to think with my mind, to love with my heart, and to speak with my lips. Since He came to seek and to save the lost, I ask Him to seek and to save the lost through me.

In the evening I ask, "Lord, is there anything in me that is displeasing to You, anything I need to confess?" If the Holy Spirit reveals any sins or weaknesses, I confess them and claim by faith God's victory for my life. I then like to spend time reading and meditating on God's Word so that my subconscious thoughts are on the Lord Jesus all during the night.

It is not always necessary to be on our knees, or even in a quiet room to pray. God wants us to be in touch with Him constantly wherever we are. We can pray in the car, while washing the dishes, or while walking down the street. The more frequently we share our thoughts and desires with our Lord, the more meaningful our fellowship and the closer we come to Him.

What Should We Include in Our Prayers?

Although prayer cannot be reduced to a formula, certain basic elements should be included in our communication with God— *Adoration, Confession, Thanksgiving, Supplication* (ACTS).

A–Adoration	To adore God is to worship and praise Him, to honor and exalt Him in our heart and mind and with our lips. The Word of God teaches that our Father desires the fellowship of His children, of which adoration is a vital part (John 4:23,24; Hebrews 12:28). Adoration expresses our complete trust in Him and reflects our confidence that He hears us. Adoration demonstrates our reverence, awe, love, and gratitude.
C–Confession	When our discipline of prayer begins with adoration, the Holy Spirit has opportunity to reveal any sin in our life that needs to be confessed. By

seeing God in His purity, His holiness, and His love, we become aware of our sinfulness and unworthiness. Confessing our sin and receiving His forgiveness restores us to fellowship with Him and clears the channel for God to hear and answer our prayers (1 John 1:7–9).

T–Thanksgiving   Nothing pleases God more than our consistent expression of faith. What better way to do this than to tell Him, "Thank You"? God's Word commands, "Give thanks in all circumstances" because "this is God's will for you in Christ Jesus" (1 Thessalonians 5:18). An attitude of thanksgiving enables us to recognize that God controls all things—not just the blessings, but the problems and adversities as well. As we approach God with a thankful heart, He becomes strong on our behalf; conversely, a critical, unbelieving spirit displeases God and hinders His efforts to bless and enrich us and to use us for His glory.

S–Supplication   Supplication includes petition for our own needs and intercession for others. We are to pray for everything and in specific terms.

As you talk to God, for example, pray that your inner person may be renewed, always sensitive to and empowered by the Holy Spirit. Pray about your problems, pray for wisdom and guidance, pray for strength to resist temptation, pray for comfort in time of sorrow—pray for everything (Philippians 4:6).

Then pray for others—your spouse, your children, your parents, neighbors, and friends. Pray for your pastor and missionaries, and for various other Christians to whom God has given special responsibility. Pray for those in authority over you (1 Timothy 2:1,2).

Pray especially for the salvation of souls, for a daily opportunity to introduce others to Christ and to the ministry of the Holy Spirit, and for the fulfillment of the Great Commission (1 Timothy 2:3,4). Begin with your campus or your community. Pray for and seek to find one or more Christian friends with whom you can establish prayer partnerships (Matthew 18:19).

These elements—*Adoration, Confession, Thanksgiving,* and *Supplication*—have helped many Christians to develop a more well-rounded prayer life.

Our Source of Power

Our power does not lie in money, genius, or dedicated work. E. M. Bounds wrote:

The Church is looking for better methods; God is looking for better men...What the Church needs today is not more or better machinery, not new organizations or more and novel methods, but men whom the Holy Ghost can use—men of prayer, men mighty in prayer. The Holy Ghost does not flow through methods, but through men. He does not come on machinery, but on men. He does not anoint plans, but men—men of prayer.

In 1954 Roger Bannister broke the four-minute mile. It had never been broken in all the centuries of recorded history, but Bannister believed it could be done. He developed a mental picture of himself breaking the record, and he did it. Since 1954, several hundred other athletes have broken the four-minute mile, simply because Roger Bannister proved that it could be done.

If an individual with only human resources is able to accomplish outstanding success, how much more can you and I do when we place our faith in the omnipotent God and draw upon His supernatural, inexhaustible resources and power?

As you carefully work through the following lessons, it is my sincere desire that you will see the importance of prayer and that you will begin immediately to spend quality time daily in such fellowship with our heavenly Father.

The Purpose of Prayer

Jesus set the perfect example of obedience in prayer. Although His day was filled from morning to night with many pressures and responsibilities—addressing crowds, healing the sick, granting private interviews, traveling, and training His disciples—He made prayer a top priority. If Jesus was so dependent upon this fellowship in prayer alone with His Father, how much more you and I should spend time alone with God.

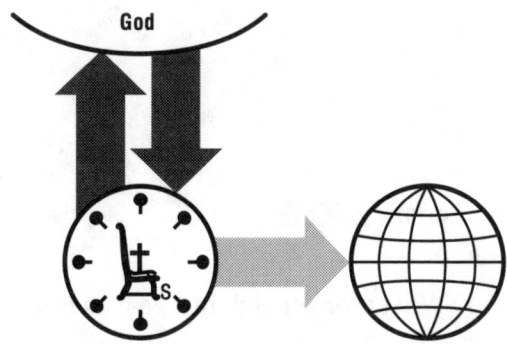

❖

Objective: To understand the importance of prayer to your Christian life

Read: Acts 3 and 4

Memorize: 1 John 5:14,15

The lives of the disciples and other Christians who have been mightily used of God through the centuries to reach their world for Christ all testify to the necessity of prayer. They too are examples of obedience to our Lord's command to pray.

Someone has wisely said, "Satan laughs at our toiling, mocks at our wisdom, but trembles when he sees the weakest saint on his knees." Prayer is God's appointed way of doing God's work.

This lesson will help you understand why prayer is so important to our Christian life. Study the lesson carefully, taking time to meditate and apply the principles you will learn.

Bible Study

Why Prayer Is Important

Read John 14:13, 1 Thessalonians 5:17, Acts 4:23–33, and Matthew 9:38.

Identify at least three reasons for prayer.

1)

2)

3)

The Apostles' Motive

Read Acts 4.

1. What problem did the apostles face?

2. Why did they not ask God to remove the persecution?

3. For what did they pray (verse 29)?

Why is this significant?

4. What was their real motive (John 14:13)?

Your Motives for Praying

On the basis of your personal experience, list at least four reasons you pray.

1)

2)

3)

4)

God's Motives In Teaching Us About Prayer

Read John 3:5–8 and John 4:23,24.

1. In what form does God exist?

What must happen to us before we can have fellowship with Him?

What kind of worship does He desire?

What is His delight (Proverbs 15:8)?

2. List some purposes of prayer from each of the following Bible references:

Matthew 7:7

Matthew 26:41

Luke 18:1

3. From your understanding of these passages, what do you think God wants you to realize about Him?

Prayer Meets the Heart's Needs

1. According to 2 Corinthians 3:5, what is the source of the Christian's sufficiency?

How do you tap into that source?

2. Read Psalm 63. Note the elements of worship and write below the word or phrase that describes how we should worship God; include references (for example, "My soul thirsts for you—Psalm 63:1").

HOW WE SHOULD WORSHIP GOD	VERSE

LIFE APPLICATION

1 What conclusions can you now make concerning your relationship with God in prayer?

2 Begin a prayer list. Keep a record of the things for which you pray.

DATE	REQUEST	DATE ANSWERED

To Whom Should We Pray?

Because the Father, Son, and Holy Spirit work in perfect unity and harmony, each has a specific role in our prayers. The writer of the Book of Hebrews said, "Let us then approach the throne of grace with confidence [boldness], so that we may receive mercy and find grace to help us in our time of need" (Hebrews 4:16).

But how do we approach the most powerful Presence in the universe? Do we pray directly to Him? Do we pray to Jesus Christ and ask Him to present our needs to the Father? How can we even approach such a holy God with boldness?

In this lesson you will learn why all three persons of the Godhead are active in our prayers and why each person performs a separate but interconnecting role.

Objective: To understand the roles of the Father, Son, and Holy Spirit in prayer

Read: Acts 5 and 6

Memorize: Philippians 4:6,7

Bible Study

To Whom Do We Pray?

1. According to Matthew 6:6, to whom should we pray?

2. From the following passages, give several reasons for your answer:

1 Chronicles 29:11,12

Matthew 6:9

John 16:23

3. Meditate on the principles contained in the following excerpt from *How to Pray* by R. A. Torrey:

> But some will say, "Is not all prayer unto God?" No. Very much so-called prayer, both public and private, is not unto God. In order that a prayer should be really unto God, there must a definite and conscious approach to God when we pray; we must have a definite and vivid realization that God is bending over us and listening as we pray.
>
> In much of our prayer there is little thought of God. Our mind is not taken up with the thought of the mighty and loving Father. We are occupied neither with the need nor with the one to whom we are praying but our mind is wandering here and there throughout the world. When we really come into God's presence, really meet Him face to face in the place of prayer, really seek the things that we desire from Him, then there is power.

How do you approach God when you pray?

How can you better focus your attention on Him?

Think about a time when you particularly sensed God's presence when you prayed. What made this time of prayer different than others?

Why?

Through Whom Do We Pray?
Read John 14:6 and 1 Timothy 2:5.

1. How many mediators are there between God and man?

Who is this mediator?

2. On the basis of Hebrews 4:14–16, describe the qualifications of our great high priest.

3. What are the requirements for a prayer relationship according to 1 John 3:21–23?

4. What does unconfessed sin in our lives do to our prayer fellowship with God (Psalm 66:18)?

5. God's Word promises in 1 John 1:9 that if we confess our sins He will forgive us. The word "confess" means to "agree with." This involves naming our sins to God, acknowledging that He has already forgiven us through Christ's death on the cross, and repenting of our sins (turning away from or changing our attitude toward them).

Follow these steps for confessing your sins:

◆ Ask the Holy Spirit to reveal any sin in your life.

◆ Write it down on a sheet of paper.

◆ Confess the sin to God and ask Him to forgive you.

◆ Receive His forgiveness by faith according to 1 John 1:9.

◆ Write the verse across the sin.

◆ Throw away the paper.

6. God honors those who truly pray in His Son's name. What is the promise recorded in John 15:16 and 16:23?

What did Jesus promise in John 14:12–14?

7. The name of Jesus means everything to God. He lifted Jesus to the highest place in the heavenly sphere and elevated His name far above all others in heaven and on earth.

From the following passages, describe the significance and standing given to the name of Jesus:

John 20:31

Acts 2:38

Acts 3:6,16; 4:10,30

Acts 19:17

Acts 4:12

Mark 9:37

Philippians 2:5–11

8. Improperly used, the name of Jesus does not bring results. To many people, the name of Jesus has become a powerless incantation, a run-together phrase, leaving them bewildered over unanswered prayer.

According to the following verses, how can we use Jesus' name properly and receive our answer from God?

1 John 5:13–15

Ephesians 5:20

Colossians 3:17

John 15:16,17

James 4:3; John 14:13

By Whom Do We Pray?

Read Ephesians 6:18 and Jude 20.

Andrew Murray, noted author and authority on prayer, wrote:

> We all admit the place the Father and the Son have in our prayer. It is to the Father we pray, and from whom we expect the answer. It is in the merit, and name, and life of the Son, abiding in Him and He in us, that we trust to be heard.
>
> But have we understood that in the Holy Trinity all the Three Persons have an equal place in prayer, and that the faith in the Holy Spirit of intercession as praying in us is as indispensable as the faith in the Father and the Son? How clearly we have this in the words, "Through Christ we have access by one Spirit to the Father."
>
> As much as prayer must be to the Father, and through the Son, it must be by the Spirit. And the Spirit can pray in no other way in us than as He lives in us. It is only as we give ourselves to the Spirit living and praying in us, that the glory of the prayer-hearing God, and the ever-blessed and most effectual mediation of the Son, can be known by us in their power.[1]

1. According to Romans 8:26,27, why does the Holy Spirit need to help us pray?

---

[1] Andrew Murray, *The Ministry of Intercession: A Plea for More Prayer* (Fleming H. Revell Company, 1898), pp. 119,120.

How does He help us pray?

Why does God answer the prayers of the Holy Spirit?

2. What, then, should be our relationship with the Holy Spirit (Ephesians 5:18)?

3. As we exercise the privilege of prayer, what does God do about our anxiety (Philippians 4:6,7)?

Give an example of how this has worked in your life.

4. Why should we cast our troubles on Him (1 Peter 5:7)?

Think back to a time when you did this. How did He answer your prayer?

What did the answer mean to you?

LIFE APPLICATION

1 List any new insights into prayer that you have gained from this lesson.

Describe how you will use these insights to have a more well-rounded prayer life.

2 Write down at least one new way in which you want to apply prayer in your life right now.

A Guide to Effective Daily Prayer

Effective prayer cannot be reduced to a magic formula. God does not respond to our requests because we have the right ritual. He is more interested in our hearts than in our words. John Bunyan, author of *Pilgrim's Progress,* said, "In prayer it is better to have a heart without words than words without a heart."

God's Word does, however, give us certain basic elements that, when included in our communication with God, will enable us to receive His answers to our prayers.

In this lesson we will consider a simple guide that you can use in your daily devotional time:

Adoration
Confession
Thanksgiving
Supplication

The guide can easily be remembered by the first letter of each word: **ACTS.**

Objective: To apply a simple guide to your daily prayer time

Read: Acts 7 and 8

Memorize: 1 Corinthians 14:40

God

Adoration
Confession
Thanksgiving
Supplication

Bible Study

Adoration

1. Why should we praise God?
Jeremiah 32:17

1 John 4:10

Philippians 1:6

2. What is the best way for you to show your gratitude toward God, and your faith and trust in Him in all circumstances (Philippians 4:6)?

What would you conclude that God expects of us (1 Thessalonians 5:16–18)?

If you sometimes find it hard to praise God, read some of the Psalms (Psalms 146–150 in particular).

3. How do you communicate your adoration to God?

Confession

Read Isaiah 59:1,2.

1. What will hinder fellowship with God?

2. Psalm 51 was David's prayer after he had fallen out of fellowship with God. What did David conclude that God wanted of him (Psalm 51:6,16,17)?

3. Read Psalm 32:1–7.
   What was David's observation about confession?

   What was his observation about not confessing his sin (verses 3,4)?

4. What should you do when you find that your fellowship with God is broken (1 John 1:9)?

   What sin in your life is keeping you from fellowship with God?

   How will you deal with that sin?

Thanksgiving

Let us never be guilty of being ungrateful to God.

1. How often should we give thanks (Hebrews 13:15)?

For what should we praise Him (Ephesians 5:20)?

Why (1 Thessalonians 5:18)?

2. What about a situation that seems adverse (Romans 5:3,4)?

3. How do you practice thankfulness when you pray?

As you go about your daily life?

4. Make a list of each problem, disappointment, heartache, or adversity that concerns you.

Begin to thank God for each one. Doing so demonstrates your trust in Him.

Supplication

1. Intercession.

An example of intercession is provided in Colossians 1:3. What was Paul's prayer for the Christians of Colosse?

Many times our efforts in leading people to Christ are fruitless because we forget the necessary preparation for witnessing. The divine order is to first talk to God about men, and then talk to men about God.

If we follow this order, we will see results. Prayer is really the place where people are won to Christ; witnessing is just gathering in the results of prayer.

As you meditate on the above, list the requests you can make to God for Christians and non-Christians.

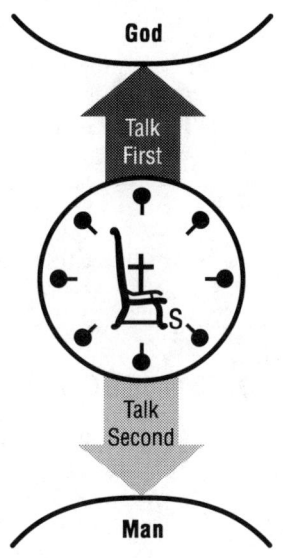

2. Petition.

Why should we expect God to answer our prayers (Matthew 7:9–11; Romans 8:32)?

According to Psalm 84:11,12, what has God promised to do?

What part does belief have in our prayers (Mark 11:24; James 1:6,7)?

Faith is necessary for answered prayers. What else is required (Matthew 6:9,10; 1 John 5:14,15)?

Why will God not answer some prayers (James 4:3)?

How does this relate to your prayer life?

3. Explain 2 Corinthians 12:7–10 in light of Romans 8:28.

What does this passage teach us about apparently unanswered prayer?

LIFE APPLICATION

1 Add other requests to the prayer list you began at the end of Lesson 1.

2 Begin using the ACTS system for prayer during your daily time alone with God. After several days, note here how your prayers have changed:

3 List daily situations in which you could use praise and thanksgiving to help you react in a godly manner.

Now follow through by applying praise and thanksgiving in these circumstances.

How to Pray With Power

Jonathan Goforth was a man of powerful prayer. It is said of him that once he felt assured of God's will in prayer, he would continue in the power of prayer until the thing was accomplished.

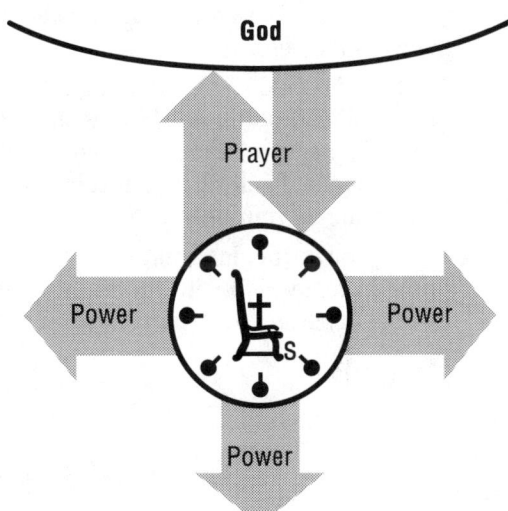

Objective: To learn how to claim by faith the great power available through prayer

Read: Acts 9 and 10

Memorize: James 5:16

Andrew Murray, too, was a great prayer warrior. He wrote in *The Praying Christian:*

The Christian needs strength. This we all know. The Christian has no strength of his own. This is also true.

Where may strength be obtained? Notice the answer: "Be strong in the Lord, and in the power of His might" (Ephesians 6:10, NKJ).

Paul had spoken of this power in the earlier part of his epistle to the Ephesians (1:18–20). He had prayed to God to give them the Spirit that they might know the exceeding greatness of His power according to the working of His mighty power, which He wrought in Christ when He raised Him from the dead.

This is the literal truth: The greatness of His power, which raised Christ from the dead, works in every believer. In me and in you, my reader. We hardly believe it, and still less do we experience it.

That is why Paul prays, and we must pray with him, that God through His Spirit would teach us to believe in His almighty power. Pray with all your heart: "Father, grant me the Spirit of wisdom, that I may experience this power in my life."

Pray for God's Spirit to enlighten your eyes. Believe in the divine power working within you. Pray that the Holy Spirit may reveal it to you, and appropriate the promise that God will manifest His power in your heart, supplying all your needs.

Do you not begin to realize that time is needed—much time in fellowship with the Father and the Son, if you would experience the power of God within you?

Bible Study

Power for Answered Prayer
Read Acts 12:5–18.

1. How did Peter's fellow Christians respond to his imprisonment (verse 5)?

What was God's answer to their prayer (verses 6–11)?

What was their response to God's answer (verses 13–16)?

How does seeing God answer your prayers in a powerful way change your feelings about prayer?

2. What do the following Bible references tell you about the qualities God demands in a person for powerful prayer?
Hebrews 11:1,6

Romans 12:1,2

Mark 11:25

1 John 3:22

Ephesians 5:18

Conditions to Answered Prayer

1. Why is it necessary to ask in accordance with the will of God (1 John 5:14,15)?

2. Write out John 15:7 in your own words and state what it teaches about conditions to answered prayer.

3. What is the value of several Christians praying for something as opposed to just one (Matthew 18:19)?

Prevailing Prayer

During his lifetime, George Mueller recorded more than 50,000 answers to prayer. He prayed for two men daily for more than 60 years. One of these men was converted shortly before Mueller's death and the other about a year later. As in Mueller's experience, we do not always see the answer to our prayers. We must leave the results to God.

One of the great needs of today is for men and women who will begin to pray for things and then pray repeatedly until they obtain what they seek from the Lord.

1. How long do you think we should pray for someone or something (Luke 18:1–8)?

Why do you think God honors prevailing prayer?

What part do our feelings play in prevailing prayer?

2. What did the following men accomplish through prayer?
Moses (Exodus 15:22–25)

Samson (Judges 16:28–30)

Peter (Acts 9:36–41)

Elijah (James 5:17,18)

3. How do these examples help you gain greater confidence
to pray?

4. Give an example of what God has done for you or someone
you know as the result of prevailing prayer.

LIFE APPLICATION

1 Examine your prayer life in light of the conditions for answered prayer. What conditions are lacking for you to have open communication with God?

How much do you really believe and trust God when you pray?

2 Write down one prayer request for which you are having to exercise "prevailing prayer."

3 List two Scripture verses that you can claim in relation to this prayer request.

1)

2)

God's Promises About Prayer

t is estimated that there are more than 5,000 personal promises in the Bible. However, these promises mean little or nothing to many Christians because they do not claim them by faith (Hebrews 4:2).

Faith is a word signifying action. For example, bags of cement sitting in a warehouse will never become concrete until they are mixed with sand, gravel, and water. Likewise, God's promises will never become concrete unless they are mixed with faith and action. You must make them yours by believing them and putting your faith to work.

❖

Objective: To claim God's promises about prayer

Read: Acts 11 and 12

Memorize: Jeremiah 33:3

This lesson will show you some of God's conditions and promises concerning prayer and His provision for your needs.

Bible Study

What God Has Promised Concerning Prayer

Look up the following verses and identify the condition and promise in each.

1. Jeremiah 33:3

Condition:

Promise:

2. Matthew 21:22

Condition:

Promise:

3. 1 John 5:14,15

Condition:

Promise:

4. John 14:14

Condition:

Promise:

5. Which promise do you need most to apply to your own prayer life right now and why?

What God Will Provide Through Prayer

In the following verses, identify God's promises concerning:
1. Material needs
Philippians 4:19

Psalm 84:11

2. Guidance
Proverbs 3:5,6

Psalm 32:8

3. Spiritual needs
Ephesians 1:3

Philippians 4:13

Why God Is Dependable

1. List reasons you can trust Him to keep His promises.
Psalm 9:10

Psalm 115:11

Isaiah 26:4

Nahum 1:7

2 Samuel 7:28

2. In what particular circumstance of your life do you presently need to trust Him more and for what?

These promises are real—believe them; claim them; live by them.

LIFE APPLICATION

List on this chart at least three things you need to pray for,
and a verse for each that promises God's provision.

NEED	PROMISE

❖   ❖   ❖

Planning Your Daily Devotional Time

Down through the years, godly men who have done great things for God have testified to the necessity of having a devotional time.

John Wesley, who shook the world for God and founded the Methodist Church, is representative of such great spiritual leaders. He thought prayer, more than anything else, to be his business.

Just as a child needs food to grow physically, so we need food to grow spiritually. We can miss a meal and not feel any ill effects, but if we don't eat for a week we begin to weaken physically. So it is in our spiritual lives.

The study of the Word of God and the practice of prayer are vitally important for spiritual growth. We may miss a day without feeding on the Word of God or praying and not feel any apparent ill effects in our lives, but if we continue this practice, we will lose the power to live the victorious Christian life.

The Christian life might be compared to a soldier in battle. He is out on the front lines but is connected with his commanding officer by radio. He calls and tells of the conditions and problems he is facing. Then his

Objective: To establish a consistent and effective daily prayer life

Read: Acts 1 and 2

Memorize: Isaiah 40:31

commanding officer, who from his vantage point can see the entire battle area, relays instructions. Similarly, the Christian shares his joys and sorrows, his victories and defeats, and his needs as God instructs and guides him through His Word.

It is our heavenly Father who directs us in the adventure of life. He knows the steps we should take. We must take time to seek Him for guidance.

Bible Study

Establish a Definite Time

A daily devotional time should be set aside for personal worship and meditation in which we seek fellowship with the Lord Jesus Christ. Once begun, this fellowship can be continued throughout the day (Psalm 119:97; 1 Thessalonians 5:17).

1. In obedience to Christ's command, what did His disciples do after His ascension (Acts 1:13,14)?

2. Although different individuals' schedules will vary, many people prefer the morning hours, before the responsibilities of the day begin.

   David was called a man after God's own heart. What time did he set aside to communicate with God (Psalm 5:3)?

Name two characteristics of the devotional life of Jesus (Mark 1:35).

1)

2)

3. When is your best devotional time?

None of us can say that we do not have time for prayer and Bible study. We all can make time for things that we really want to do. Whether the period is long or short, set aside some time.

4. Make your devotional time unhurried. Don't think about your next responsibility. Concentrate on your fellowship with the Lord. A definite time every day will do much to help. A brief period with concentration is better than a long devotional time with your mind on many things.

How many minutes can you set aside daily for your time with God?

Choose a Definite Place

Avoid distraction by finding a quiet, private place of worship. If privacy is impossible, you will need to learn to concentrate. If you cannot have a devotional time in your own home or room, perhaps one of the following places will be suitable:

◆ A nearby chapel

◆ A corner of the school library

◆ Your office (before or after hours)

Name three other places you might find appropriate for your private prayer and Bible study.

1)

2)

3)

Goal and Content of the Devotional Time

1. We should have a reason for everything we do. "Aim at nothing and you will surely hit it." Our purpose for prayer should be to establish personal fellowship with God and to fulfill our own spiritual needs.

   A brief time of meeting with God in the early morning and walking in vital union with Him throughout the day, "practicing the presence of God," is more meaningful than spending an hour or more in a legalistic way and forgetting Him for the rest of the day.

   During our devotional time, we should be concerned with learning where we have failed and with rededicating ourselves to the task before us. We should use the time to regroup our forces after the battles of the previous day and plan for the next day's attack.

   What particular spiritual need do you feel today?

   What battles did you have yesterday?

2. The devotional time should include Bible study, prayer, personal worship, and quiet meditation. These aspects of the devotional time are so closely related that you can actually engage in all at the same time.

   For example, begin by reading a psalm of thanksgiving or praise. As you read, your heart will respond and you will continue to praise and worship God from a grateful heart.

   Turn now to another portion of Scripture, such as Romans 8. Interrupt your reading to thank God for each truth that applies to you as a Christian. You will be amazed at how much you have to praise and thank God for, once you get started.

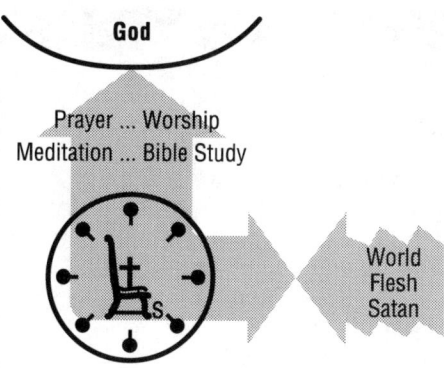

After you have read and prayed for a while, remain in an attitude of quiet, listening for instructions from God. Write down any thoughts that come to mind and pray about these.

Supplementary activity may include memorizing Scripture or reading from a devotional book or hymnal.

3. Study Matthew 6:9–13. Paraphrase this prayer in your own words, using expressions meaningful to you.

For additional information on prayer, see my Transferable Concept, *How You Can Pray With Confidence.*

LIFE APPLICATION

Complete these statements:

1 I have set aside the following definite time in the day for daily devotional time:

2 I have decided on the following place:

3 My purpose for setting aside a definite time and place for my devotions is to:

4 I will include the following activities during my devotional time:

Recap

The following questions will help you review this Step. If necessary, reread the appropriate lesson(s).

1. Why is prayer so important?

2. To be more effective in prayer, what conditions mentioned in Lessons 4 and 5 are you now meeting that you weren't meeting before?

3. Fill in the words to complete the suggested guide for prayer content:

A

C

T

S

Reread: Acts 13 and 14

Review: Verses memorized

LIFE APPLICATION

1 Are you presently following the ACTS guide? (Remember, a guide is not mandatory, it is just helpful.)

If you use another system, what is it?

2 How has your understanding of power and promises in prayer been broadened?

3 What specific time and place have you set aside for daily prayer and devotions?

Time:

Place:

What adjustments do you need to make for it to be more effective (more or less time, different place, etc.)?

4 Memorize and remember:

Effective praying is simply asking God to work according to His will and leaving the results to Him.

Ten Basic Steps Toward Christian Maturity

Eleven easy-to-use individual guides to help you understand the basics of the Christian faith

A Time-Tested Study Series Featuring:

INTRODUCTION: The Uniqueness of Jesus
Explains who Jesus Christ is, His earthly life, His death and resurrection, and His continuing ministry in the lives of all believers. Reveals the secret of His power to turn you into a victorious, fruitful Christian.

STEP 1: The Christian Adventure
Shows you how to enjoy what millions of other Christians around the world have experienced—the adventure of a full, abundant, purposeful, and fruitful life in Christ.

STEP 2: The Christian and the Abundant Life
Explores the Christian way of life—what it is and how it works practically. Discusses the problems of temptation, sin, and spiritual warfare. Points the way to victorious living.

STEP 3: The Christian and the Holy Spirit
Teaches who the Holy Spirit is, how to be filled with the Spirit, and how to make the Spirit-filled life a moment-by-moment reality in your life. The truths you learn will ignite your spirit.

STEP 4: The Christian and Prayer
Shows how to fellowship with God and receive His answers to your prayers. Reveals the true purpose of prayer and shows how the Father, Son and Holy Spirit work together to answer your prayers. You will discover how to use the great power of prayer effectively.

STEP 5: The Christian and the Bible
Talks about the Bible—how we got it, its authority, and its power to help the believer. Offers methods for studying the Bible more effectively. Shows how to claim God's promises to you as a believer.

STEP 6: The Christian and Obedience

Learn why it is so important to obey God and how to live daily in His grace. Discover the secret to personal purity and power as a Christian and why you need not fear what others think of you.

STEP 7: The Christian and Witnessing

Shows you how to witness effectively in the power of the Holy Spirit and how to know when He is leading you in sharing your faith. Includes a reproduction of the *Four Spiritual Laws* and explains how to share them. Follow the proven concepts of this Step and you will develop confidence to share Christ as a way of life.

STEP 8: The Christian and Giving

Offers sound biblical principles for giving that will enable you to enjoy the promised blessings of God in your life. Discover God's plan for your financial life, how to stop worrying about money, and how to trust God for your finances.

STEP 9: Exploring the Old Testament

Features a brief survey of the Old Testament, including key events, concepts and characters. Shows what God did to prepare the way for Jesus Christ and the redemption of all who receive Him as Savior and Lord. Reveals God's pattern of promise and blessing and explores the true significance of God's grace and forgiveness.

STEP 10: Exploring the New Testament

Reviews each of the New Testament books and contains a brief survey of their contents. Shows the essence of the gospel and highlights the exciting beginning of the Christian church.

Leader's Guide

The ultimate resource for even the most inexperienced, timid and fearful person asked to lead a group study in the basics of the Christian life. No more fumbling for answers. Contains insets revealing both questions and answers from the *Ten Step Study Guides*.

A Handbook for Christian Maturity

Combines the eleven-booklet series into one practical, easy-to-follow volume. Excellent for personal or group study.

Available through your local Christian bookstore, mail-order catalog distributor, or NewLife Publications.

Notes

About the Author

BILL BRIGHT is founder and president of Campus Crusade for Christ International. Serving in 152 major countries representing 98 percent of the world's population, he and his dedicated associates of nearly 50,000 full-time staff, associate staff, and trained volunteers have introduced tens of millions of people to Jesus Christ, discipling millions to live Spirit-filled, fruitful lives of purpose and power for the glory of God.

Dr. Bright did graduate study at Princeton and Fuller Theological seminaries from 1946 to 1951. The recipient of many national and international awards, including five honorary doctorates, he is the author of numerous books and publications committed to helping fulfill the Great Commission. His special focus is New Life 2000, an international effort to help reach more than six billion people with the gospel of our Lord Jesus Christ and help fulfill the Great Commission by the year 2000.